Parade Readying Your Horse

American Sidesaddle Association

Written by Gael Orr, Vicki Pritchard, Maggie Herlensky, and Audrey Sears

Parade Readying your Horse

By American Sidesaddle Association
Copyright 2022 American Sidesaddle Association

Cover Photo by Jennifer Roger

All rightes reserved. No part of the guide may be used or reproduced in any manner without the written premissions of the author/publisher/illustrator.

Publisher's Cataloging-in-Publication Data

American Sidesaddle Association, 2008 -
      Parade Readying your Horse

ISBN 978-1-940843-10-0
1. Horsemanship - Sidesaddle Riding 2. Horses - Showing
3. Horsemanship - Competitions - Show Riding 4. Horsemanship - Riding Etiquette 5. Horse sports

Parade History
by
Audrey Black

"I love a Parade, the tramping of feet; I love every beat I hear of a drum." The lyrics of the Arden & Ohman song always ring in my ears when I think of the fanfare that comes along with a parade. Other than enjoying the sights and smells and the events that precede or follow a parade, do you really know much about them?

Parades can be dated back well into 2000 BC. These were mostly processions celebrating events. This could be for religious, political, I or even personal reasons. In its most basic form a "procession of people." Hunters returning from a hunt, nobility, religious ceremonies, and military displays are all examples of early parades. According to the Merriam-Webster Dictionary the word "parade" comes from a French word meaning "to prepare." The word showed up in the mid-1600's. It was used to refer to "a pompous show" or "an exhibition."

A parade started to refer to "a ceremonial formation of a body of troops before a superior officer;" this continues to be the most well-known use and definition of the word. Today parades still are held to celebrate events, significant dates, and even religious purposes. They still maintain a "procession of people" and often, motorized vehicles and even animals perform "a procession" or "a pompous show" on a particular theme or common cause.

Lyrics: https://www.allthelyrics.com/lyrics/arden_ohman/i_love_a_parade-lyrics-268957.html

Merriam-Webster Dictionary: https://www.merriam-webster.com/words-at-play/parade-the-words-history-on-parade#:~:text=It%20comes%20to%20English%20from,a%20pompous%20show%2C%20an%20exhibition.

Early Parades by History Daily: https://historydaily.org/parade-history-when-did-we-start-doing-this-all-the-time#:~:text=For%20most%20of%20ancient%20history,own%20king%2C%20strangely%20enough).

Parade Readying the Side Saddle Horse
by
Gael Orr

When I (Gael Orr) was a young teenager, I used to ride my horse in our community's Nunda Fundays parade every year. I enjoyed it tremendously. It was an opportunity to get my horse looking beautiful for all the admirers in my small town. I grew up in the Village of Nunda, New York, with a population of about 800 people, and 2,000 cows.

As an adult I wanted to ride in parades, but the parade training always held me back. I think at the age of 14 I wasn't so worried if my horse could handle it or not (I bounced a lot better then, if I did take a fall). The concerns of past experiences dealing with an emotional horse and my worrying mind (considering all the things that could go wrong) simply held me back from even trying.

Last year, I rode in Gettysburg at the Remembrance Day Parade, borrowing my girlfriend's horse. I had such an amazing "mountain top" experience, that I wanted the feeling to last. I don't mind sharing that I've been through a lot over the last ten years, and happiness has been elusive. I've had to make happiness a cognitive choice, so It was extra special for me to have a parade experience deliver such delicious moments of unabated joy. Simply put, that moment inspired me to figure out how to get my personal horse trained for parades.

Last October, I got a new horse. I named her Bunny. She's

an off-track standardbred, and a little bit older at 17. I didn't think I'd ever be saddle training a horse again, but there I was, crushing it, taking on a horse with only 10 mounted rides before I got her. My ultimate goal for parade riding is to ride my horse, Bunny, sidesaddle. Now, I recognize many of you may not be that interested in riding sidesaddle. That's okay, this guide is also for you. My ultimate objective for writing this, is to help people who want to ride in parades. Hopefully you will ride as safely as possible, and come to understand how you can support your horse through that training journey. When it comes to riding sidesaddle, remember, anything you can do riding astride, you can do riding aside, except for roping and playing polo!

1. Evaluate your horse
2. Desensitize
3. Find the right support horses
4. Temper Your expectations
5. Take your time

Evaluate your Horse

I think the key consideration for figuring out what kind of horse you want to ride in a parade, you have to look at the horse itself. Do you have the right horse for a parade? Bunny has a great mind, she's very caring, wants to please, and is quite brave. I have a barn full of horses, 7 actually. But other than my little pony Pumpkin, I had little confidence that any of my current horses could handle a parade. While I hoped my mare, Ivy, could manage it, she was nursing an injury that made her recovery uncertain. (I'm delighted to report, she's made a full recovery, and is in parade training as we speak!) Another one of my horses, Sam, a paint cob, while adorable, is really pretty stupid, acts unpredictably at times, and when he comes unglued, he doesn't care who's in his way. Clearly he's not a good parade candidate. My other horse, Reime, is a Lusitano, quite hot, and he used to have a pretty bad rearing problem. He will never be a sidesaddle mount and share my key goal to ride in parades aside. Eventually, he was eliminated as a suitable parade choice.

Evaluating your horse's potential is important. Can any horse be parade trained? Maybe...probably not. Is every horse capable of being a mounted police horse? No. Not every horse can handle lots of stimulation. If you believe that any horse could be parade trained, I challenge you by asking how much time, energy, and investment do you want to make to insure that can happen? What should you look for; how do you evaluate the right horse for the job? I would say, pick a mare or gelding for the job and leave your stallion at home. Most large parades don't allow stallions. If you do have a stallion that could handle a parade, then you have a lot of extra things to consider, along with placement in the actual parade itself. I'd say, you probably want the stallion to be the first horse in the line up, ahead of any mares, and not the last horse in a lineup of horses. If there is a mare in season at a parade, it could be an extremely dangerous situation for everyone. But I digress. Let's discuss temperament.

I think what you want to consider is, how brave is your horse, and how can you tell if he or she is brave? My horse Bunny is a horse that will walk past nearly anything that upsets her without freaking out in such a way that is unmanageable. She might shy a bit around the object and give it a weird look, but she's willing to push past the object. A curious horse is a good thing, too. Is your horse willing to sniff something that it is nervous about without bolting? I find a horse that is a tad on the lazy side is a nicer horse to train for parades, too. There is something about a carefree disposition that can be invaluable.

Choosing a horse that isn't a hotblood (thoroughbreds and arabians) as a general rule can make your training go faster. That's not to say you can't use these breeds, it just may take more time to train them. And every horse is uniquely different of course, so you have to consider each horse individually. But in general, choosing a calmer horse is a good idea. If your horse is one that prances in place a lot, or is emotionally excitable, parades may not be in their repertoire. Selecting a horse that stands quietly is really important, too, because when you are in a parade you have to halt and stand frequently. When it comes to parades, the halt is the most important gait.

So for me, my parade horse became my mare, Bunny. I had just gotten her and I wasn't sure she could cut it at first. She seemed a little spooky when I first got her. What changed my mind about her, was that in spite of her fears, she always pushed through them anyway, wasn't explosive, and looked to me for support. If something scared her, she would shy a bit around the object, but didn't actually spook, bolt, jump, rear, buck, or do anything stupid. She'd look at it with a "hairy eyeball," and breathe funny, but kept going by walking a little faster. Perfect!

De-sensitivity Training

The first thing I did with Bunny, was start to desensitize her. I used small flags, large flags, and made lots of noises. I even purchased an extremely obnoxious kids' police siren (that I might re-gift to someone's child who annoys me) that had flashing lights to get her exposed to lights and siren noises. I did that for about a month, very consistently, and our training sessions were very short, three times a week for 10-15 minutes. I kept the training sessions short, but frequent. And I didn't go crazy with the de-sensitivity training either. I did the best I could.

Our first parade was the Dansville Winter in the Village Christmas Parade. I chose this parade because it was super short in length, just one block long, had a fire truck in it, that was silent, and had one marching band in it. If all hell broke loose, I didn't want to be in a two mile long parade. I asked my grandson to ride our pony Pumpkin. She's a little bomb proof mare that I had no doubt would be just fine, although she had never been in a parade before. I'd seen Pumpkin stand next to the road when firetrucks went past my farm and she didn't care. I mean, the world could crash down on this pony, and she just wouldn't care. I also knew she would be fine in crowds from all the horse shows she's done in her lifetime. She became my support horse. In that very first parade, my friend Audrey loaned us her parade trained horse, Fancy Nancy that my friend Suzzanna rode. So we had two solid support horses for my untrained mare.

Support Horses

I think it's really important to have an already parade trained horse in your parade line-up. I had my friend's horse Fancy-Nancy gave support to all the other horses in our line-up, including my little bomb proof pony Pumpkin. I recommend finding someone who already has a parade trained horse, and ride with them because horses feed off of each other's energy. Having a confident horse or two next to yours makes a huge difference in being successful.

How do I know this? I actually looked into police trained horses. I was looking at their training, and even considered hosting a workshop. What they do to get their horses ready for all of the stimulation they undergo, is train horses in groups. Afterall, horses are herd animals. They use solid well-trained horses to train greener ones. Check out their website: http://www.mountedpolicetrainingacademy.com/

In the first parade, my friend Debbie also rode with me on her horse, also a bomb proof wonder-boy and she brought her grandson on his equally bomb proof pony mare. (Neither horse had been in a parade before, but they had the right temperament and we had Fancy Nancy to support the rest.) So that first parade, we had four horses that had never been in a parade, three of which were bomb proof horses, and one horse that was a seasoned parade horse. Get a good horse support team.

Temper Your Expectations

Be a good support person to your horse. I went to the parade with ZERO expectations that we would be successful. I adjusted my attitude to this: If she has a melt down and can't handle the commotion, I'll put her back on the trailer and do more desensitization work at home. If she is upset, but handling it and jigging a bit, I'll hand walk her through the parade. If she is a little anxious, but doing well, I'll have my husband clip a lead rope onto her, and ride through with him as a side walker. And if she is having no issues at all, I'll just ride her through the parade. The key thing here is I had no expectations that I had to ride her through the parade, or that she would be successful. I was there to support my horse in any state in which she presented herself, and to help her through it.

Our second parade was the very next day and it was a horses only parade. I'm delighted to report, I was able to ride her through with a side walker. A siren went off while she was tied to the horse trailer, and she didn't care, not even a little. That made me feel a lot better as it's the sirens, marching bands, balloon carts, (sun or rain) umbrellas, and loud noises that made me wonder how a horse can handle it all at the same time. In fact, in Bunny's third parade, I rode her in a huge parade, and she was fine through the entire thing. Then as I was walking her back to the parade start, she shied at a stationary mailbox. Gotta love horses! Guess what, she was worse at the horses only parade, than the one the day before that had all the stimulation. Sometimes in training, horses get a little worse, then get a lot better. With hindsight, maybe two parade days in a row was a bit much for her.

Take Your Time

Our third parade, I didn't need a side walker at all, but my husband still walked alongside of me with a rope in hand, just in case I needed him. I still had my support pony Pumpkin ridden by a friend. Pumpkin has been in every parade with Bunny, giving Bunny the emotional support she needs.

Our fourth parade, I introduced my horse Ivy. Ivy rode paired next to Pumpkin. She exhibited no issues whatsoever. Not one! She didn't need a side walker, she walked calmly down the parade route next to Pumpkin like she'd done parades every day of her life. Ivy was next to Pumpkin, with Bunny right behind her. She had the confidence of her herd to draw upon. I have yet to ride her sidesaddle in any of these parades, but I will in time. I'm in no rush, I'm taking my time to get the training right. I want to make sure my horses are in a good mental place before I tax them further with another thing to think about (carrying me aside).

Desensitization

Desensitizing your horse is really all about your imagination. This is an important step to getting your horse ready for parades. Make no mistake about it, I worked on desensitizing my horses before I put them in any parade. Get creative. What kinds of things do your horses react to, and how can you help them get used to that stimulation? The objective isn't just about exposing your horses to things you know they may fear, although that helps. Really the key thing to desensitizing your horse, is about teaching your horse to be able to handle things they don't understand, to turn to you for comfort and guidance, and to work through their issues. For example, how could you simulate in training having to walk your horse past a line up of 25 antique tractors that are growling and sputtering and backfiring? You can't! But what you can do, is get them used to weird noises and objects so that if you are faced with a tractor line up, they know how to handle themselves. Here are a few ideas you can start to work through. You can use my list as an idea list, and add to it as you go! This list is in no particular order or priority.

Environmental Conditioning

Take your horse to a village, and ride around the community. Guaranteed, kids will come out to want to pet your horse, baby strollers may go by, dogs will yap, car doors will slam, a bicycle will go by, or a motorcycle...riding around a village is a great thing to do. Take your horse somewhere where you can tie them up and get some food or ice cream. Letting them be tied, while there is mild commotion going on, is the first step to getting them to tie nicely when there is a lot more commotion going on. Take your horse to a friend's farm, and expose them to different sights and sounds.

Find a community parade that you can participate in. Often a local museum may have a historical reenactment parade that doesn't have fire trucks, honking horns, revving sports cars, and other loud stimulation. Typically you'd find a drum line with a fife and lots of people. This is a great first parade. Or pick a horse parade, or create one yourself. Invite your friends to ride around a community and sing Christmas Carols. Ask if you can attend a 5K race with your horse, and stand on a corner on the runner route, and wave to the runners as they go by. Ask yourself, who already has parade trained horses with whom you could participate in a parade? If you come up with nothing, and don't actually know anyone, is there a local horse association that you might join that engages in parades? What about your local fox hunting club? Many actually do a parade down their town's Main Street with all the hounds. Maybe you could join them?

Other places to ride your horse could include a junkyard. Ride past a junkyard. Lots of times, old dairy farms have tons of junk lying around that you can ride by. Cemeteries make another great place to ride around, just make sure you pick up any droppings or take a friend to be on the ground. There's nothing like lots of "rocks" to ride around to desensitize your horse. Some other fun ideas are to take your horse to a local park and go trail riding. Participate in a local horse show, hunter pace, or fox hunting event. Some of my friends trailer their horses to events like these, not to participate by riding in them, but solely to give their horses some exposure to those environments. Why not host your own clinic? Host a mounted police training event on your farm. Another idea for exposure is take your horse to a feed mill where they have weighing stations and weigh your horse on their scales. This is an opportunity for noise desensitization and "bridge" simulation of uneven surfaces.

Give your horse exposure to other horses under saddle to correct any "fighting." My horse is a mare (I know, I can hear your eyes rolling from here). And let's face it, some mares like to kick other horses. Getting them desensitized and having the ability to correct any of those habits before a parade, is a good idea. Zero tolerance for horse fights and mating rituals during parades, I say!

Be able to train your horse to trailer load, with and without tack. I know this is controversial. Some people don't like to load horses wearing tack, but let me present you with this idea. What if you go to a parade, and your horse has a meltdown, and you have to get them on the trailer fast to get them safe? You may not have time to tie up and untack the horse. Having them able to load onto a trailer while carrying a saddle is a good idea. You can strip their tack after they are secure if you want.

Another key safety tip for training your horse, is to really dial in the one-rein stop. YouTube has lots of videos for one-rein stop. By practicing that really well with your horse, you'll have the right tool to use in the event your horse spooks badly. Turning your horse into a tight circle, can really help keep you safe too. For sidesaddle riders, make sure you have that dialed in turning to the left side. If your sidesaddle horse spooks bent to the right, you can still spin your horse around, but you won't have the benefit of your right let to assist you. Having your one-rein stop well practiced in a controlled environment will really help you in the event of an emergency. Train your horse to understand the one-rein stop.

Training

Some noise training and visual alarms desensitization ideas are:

- Umbrellas - visual
- Billowing skirts- visual and tactile
- Marching bands, snare drums, - visual, and sound
- Snappers (kids toss them on the ground)- visual, sound, smell
- Flags- large color guard style-visual, sound
- Small flags-visual
- Balloons-visual
- Balloons popping-sound
- Sirens- sound
- Strollers-visual and sound
- Vender carts- strategy: use strollers with lots of junk on them to simulate venders pushing carts down the street- visual and sound
- Mascots and clowns- visual
- Go-karts- visual and sound
- Traffic
- Applause- sound
- Kids screaming/crying- sound
- Amusement park ride noises
- Fireworks noises
- Gun shots

- Flares
- Toy rattlesnake noise and shaking
- Plastic bags
- Flashing lights
- Bagpipes
- Confetti tossing
- Tractors pulling wagons
- Loudspeaker announcements
- Dragging items around while leading the horse- sound, visual
- Strategy: Airhorn/Sirens- use this method for calling in horses for nighttime feeding
- Llamas, sheep, goats, cows, & dogs
- Screaming children
- Throwing candy (toss it off your horse, toss it at your horse, toss it in front of your horse, behind your horse... you get the idea, toss candy!)

Smells
Sulfur- flares and snappers
Food smells

Footing
Gravel, Concrete, asphalt, dirt, brick. (they make different sounds)
Puddles
Paint that are on crosswalks and center lines, manhole covers, grates
Bridges-grated

Preparing for your Parade

When your horse is ready for its first parade, find the parade that you want to do, and know where you are going. Be sure to ask for an address, or key landmark for the parade line-up. Make sure when you attend your first parade that you contact the event coordinator, and fill out their registration paperwork. They may require insurance, most do not. They may require you to have a pooper-scooper person on the course, most do not, but it is the right thing to do, anyway. Cleaning up along the parade route is considerate, and will help get you invited to return to their parade in the future. Ask also where trailer parking is, as that might not be at the parade line-up.

I attended a parade once where the parking lot was too small for my trailer. The parade director had never had horses in their parade before and didn't realize fully hitched up that I was over 40 feet long! Ask the question of the parade coordinator where trailer parking is, and what kind of turn around space you might have. Don't be afraid to make recommendations for parking locations if you know the neighborhood well. Often coordinators don't consider the number and sizes of horse trailers.

I hope it goes without saying to make sure that your horse is clean and presentable to ride in any parade. It's the rider's responsibility to make sure the horse they are riding is bathed and groomed before the parade or any rehearsal and/or meeting. Make sure your tack is also cleaned, and not faded or with rusty buckles. If you are riding western, then you want to make sure your bridle has a noseband because you are in a very stimulated environment, and having a noseband on your horse can help your side walker in the event they need to get a fast hand on your horse. If your horse is not a steady parade horse, place a halter under the bridle. Thus a strong place is provided for a sidewalker to hold onto, and to clip on a lead rope if needed. If you are riding aside, only sidesaddles with leaping horns should be used. If an individual is leasing a horse, they should arrive on time to get the horse ready. It is also considerate to contribute to fuel reimbursement if trailer hauling was not part of the lease fee.

If you are riding in a group and there is a mounted rehearsal and safety briefing, being on time is vital. As a rider you will receive your riding position and instruction. At a parade meeting or rehearsal, a rider will be given their line up position. Please respect that this is based on certain criteria and may change from time to time as new horses and riders are added. Positions are based on safety, and a solid team appearance. If there is a safety concern, a rider is welcome to bring it up with the parade coordinator. If asking to swap positions, both riders must be in agreement, and present it to the parade coordinator. The riders must respect the coordinator's final decision. It's super helpful to your horse to put one experienced parade rider in each row. Once on the parade route, please listen to this rider. It is understood that even solid parade horses can have a bad day. However, the harder all riders work to be a team, the better the unit looks. All these things can be practiced at home with a few friends.

When riding in your parade as an individual, or as a group, there are a lot of safety considerations. Not just for yourself and your horse, but also for the public. For your first few parades, I can't stress enough the importance of a side walker. They are there to clip a rope onto your horse and lead you through the parade, or clip onto your horse in the event of an emergency. Something worth noting about side walkers, is that it can be really good for your horse, if you have someone side walking that has a relationship with your horse. Often my husband will walk alongside our horses on a parade route. He helps with farm chores and feeds our horses. One of his strategies with a new horse that we are parade-training, is that if the horse is reasonably calm, and not in need of having him clip on rope, he positions himself just in front of the horse. By walking slightly ahead of the horse, this too gives the horse comfort. The horse is now following someone it trusts. This too can relax a horse and give them some extra support, without being led by a rope.

Side walkers are also in charge of keeping people from approaching you too closely. The side walker keeps the horse from backing into the crowd and warns the spectators to stay back. He or she is your own personal safety guide. I can't tell you how many people want to come pet your horse. Many are wearing flip flops or sandals, or are tiny children that shouldn't be approaching your horse at all. And this happens at the parade lineup, as well as when you are going down the street. When people ask if they can pet my horse, I look at their shoes first. If they aren't wearing the right ones, I just tell them, "I'm sorry, I can't let you do that, your footwear isn't secure enough and I'd hate for my horse to accidentally step on you." Most people never even consider that and actually thank me for saying as much. During the parade if someone asks to pet my horse, "I just politely say, "Thank you for asking. Stand back please. I don't want my horse to step on you." I encourage good vocal interaction with the crowd. Talk to people as you ride by and definitely wave. But do not allow people to interact with your horse, and do not ride next to the crowds. Keep your horse in the center of the street!
Pay attention to yourself and your horse. It's better to be safe than sorry. If you're uncomfortable in a parade let a side walk-

er know you need their support. It is completely acceptable for you to dismount and hand-walk your horse in a parade. If your horse is getting upset this is no place to school them. Let a side walker know you need their help so they can clip onto your horse, and possibly help you dismount if needed.

It's also a good idea to also have someone who pushes a wheelbarrow and shovel or rake, through the parade to clean up after your horse. As a general rule, I try to leave a parade as clean as I found it. That may also mean you should carry a broom where your trailer is parked. The clean up person should also show good sportsmanship and pick up after any other horses in the parade, too, not just the ones that belong to your team. It's not uncommon to find mounted police patrols at the parades; and yes, we clean up after their horses too!

Once you've experienced several parades and your horse has performed quietly and is in good emotional control, it would then be an acceptable time to try a parade aside. I recommend that when you ride sidesaddle for the first time in a parade, pick a parade that is quieter and smaller. Just like when you introduced your horse to parades initially, with patience and training, so should you also do for sidesaddle riding. A historical reenactment parade is an excellent choice, as typically you don't get as much noise and commotion. If you are doing historical reenactment, you can purchase a vintage safety bowler online. Typically eBay has them. They aren't as good as an ASTM helmet, but they are better than having no helmet at all. Some historical reenactments prefer riders not wear modern safety gear. But wear a helmet anyway. And if you feel that you don't want to spoil your look, a safety derby is a good secondary option, or a velvet helmet.

The first time you ride aside in a parade, it's a good idea to have a side walker present, and latched onto your horse. It's recommended that you always put a halter on under your bridle so as to affix a rope to it should the need arise. Halter bridles are also a good option for parades. By putting the halter on under the bridle, this won't interfere with your reins while you ride.

Be in no rush with your horse's training either. It's perfectly acceptable to spend months training your horse for parades, maybe even a year or more, before riding aside. Again, eliminate any expectations, and move at the speed and pace of your horse's emotional ability and maturity. If your horse does get upset or begins to show signs of an emotional meltdown, dismount immediately, and hand walk the horse. If you can do so safely, remove the horse from the parade. Listen to the horse. Some people may think they should just try and "ride it out" but honestly, that's just a good way of getting hurt or hurting someone else. Listen to your horse, and do what is best for the horse. Some larger parades may even have veterinary services that can assist you with a mild sedation if the horse has a "nuclear" meltdown.

When you are ready to ride aside in a parade, remember to wear a safety apron. If you decide to wear a skirt, it should be full enough to drape safely around sidesaddle horns.. You may open a seam and add velcro for extra safety. You may use a matching apron and pretty top instead of a dress. When riding in a sidesaddle skirt or safety apron, make sure the toe of your left foot is covered, while your right foot should be completely covered. The hem should be level and weighted, so it doesn't blow in the wind. Safety aprons should be able to rip free of the rider in the unlikely event of a fall. Velcro is your friend. You do not want to get entangled in your skirt if you have to dismount quickly or get tossed off. Circle skirts should have a seam on the right side that can Velcro shut. Also, under your safety skirt or apron, be sure to wear breeches, not historical bloomers or anything slippery. I recommend you wear the same color breeches as your skirt. Make sure you are using a safety release stirrup for the sidesaddle. Double check your tack before mounting up, and make sure you aren't wearing anything that could get you strangled, like a scarf, in the unlikely event that things go wrong. Once you really start getting into parades you may find you are working with a group of friends or a team. Often a group may designate a costume coordinator. It's fun to match your friends in a parade, or all dressed to a theme. We often do this for Memorial Day parades dressed in red, white, and blue.

If you are in costume, make sure that your costume is comfortable. Give your costume a test drive at home. You don't want the first time you try on your costume to be in a parade, because if you do need to adjust something, you may need the time to do so. What if you are wearing a long skirt and your horse wigs out over how it blows in the breeze? You probably don't want to make that discovery, and have that horse's fear intensify at the same time as a firetruck blows off a crowd pleasing siren. The same is true of your tack. You want to know how your equipment is going to feel, how your horse will respond to both tack and costumes is helpful. Set yourself up for success and try out your tack and equipment at home.

Once on the parade route, maintain your assigned position. Try and make sure that your horse stays in alignment if riding tandem or next to another horse. If you are riding single file, be sure to keep a horse length distance between horses. The horse length is determined by the size of the horse one is riding. The bigger the horse you are personally riding, the bigger your distance needs to be. If a spectator approaches you as a rider, be sure to politely ask them to step back away from your horse. As you ride down the parade route, you should remain as close to the center of the road as you can for the safety of spectators. Plus, if your horse does spook, having as much space as possible between you and the crowd is helpful. Safety walkers will also help to keep you and spectators safe.

I hope your biggest take-away from all of this parade education, is that parade training is really about being as supportive as possible to your equine friend, and helping them through some challenges. Everything about a parade assaults their senses. I can think of fewer other opportunities where you can provide an environment that can be so amazingly helpful at desensitizing your horse. Parades are arguably the best possible way to "bomb proof" your horse. Also, parades are an incredible opportunity for you to deepen your bond with your horse. As you continue to parade train your horse, you are teaching your horse to come to you for comfort and help.

Remember

1. Evaluate your horse
2. Desensitize
3. Find the right support horses
4. Temper your expectations
5. Take your time

Readying the Rider

Overview

1. Acknowledge your emotions
2. Determine what your inner dialogue is
3. Change the inner dialogue with a mantra
4. Have patience as our brain readjusts to our new thoughts and triggers a new emotion

What kind of guide would this be, if we didn't touch on rider anxiety? First, a small disclaimer. I'm not a psychologist, but I do know something about emotional intelligence, and how to control our inner narrative. I'm hoping these tips may help you, if you are one of those nervous-Nellies when it comes to riding. Rider anxiety is no joke, and guess what, parades can be just as emotionally taxing to the rider as to your horse. In fact, people get so keyed up, they get into a panicky state. Your horse will definitely mimic that fear. New studies show that horses actually reflect our emotions, and can read our facial expressions. They hear our heartbeat from four feet away, and respond to our tone of voice. And according to Medical News Today, horses find "baby-talk" to be relaxing.

Parades present an uncontrollable environment, and this can cause a rider to have anxiety, especially the first parade that you attend with your horse. If you're like me, you probably are considering all the things that could go wrong. We don't want spectators, our horse, or ourselves to get hurt. Parades are supposed to be fun and enjoyable. Listen to your horse. By eliminating your expectations of success, and going with the attitude of helping your horse, you'll take the pressure off of yourself!

Here are some of the secrets of emotional control. It sounds great on paper, it is hard to do in everyday life, and it takes practice. Here is the good news, you can practice emotional control, daily. Here are a few secrets about emotional intelligence (EQ). Every emotion a person experiences is triggered by a thought. If you are in a rage, there is an internal story you are telling yourself, that is causing that emotion. If you are experiencing fear, or sadness, it's the same thing. A thought has triggered your brain to fire off chemicals to create an emotional response. The exchange between emotions and thoughts are so fast, you may not realize you had a thought that triggered the emotional response, in the first place. And in fact, there is such a thing as a conditioned response. This can happen when you have experienced a traumatic emotion in the past. When you experience some similar stimulation, the emotional reaction is instantly triggered. You see this in post-traumatic stress experiences. So our first step in understanding our emotions, is to acknowledge them. So when you are feeling an emotion, your first step, is to simply observe your emotions.

For example, let's say you get to the parade line up, and you get scared. You observe your emotion, which in this case is fear. Now, ask yourself why you are afraid. What internal dialogue are you telling yourself? Asking yourself what your story is, is the second step in changing how you feel about something. So let's say in this case you are telling yourself, "I'm afraid if I get on my horse, and try and ride in this parade, my horse will freak out and throw me." So you are afraid you will fall off. The internal dialogue you are telling yourself is if you get on your horse, you will fall. That thought is triggering the emotion, fear. The speed of emotions can be so fast, sometimes you have to try and figure out why you are reacting emotionally, in the first place. That is why I say, observe your emotions, then get cranial about this, and think about and ask yourself what are you telling yourself? Emotions can be so fast, it may take you several minutes to unpack why you are feeling something in the first place. Emotional reactions are created in the brain as a matter of survival. Your exposure to past experiences can elicit a conditioned emotional response. So unpacking those feelings, observing them, asking yourself why you are feeling them, and what you are thinking, can take a bit of practice and time.

If you can change your internal dialogue, you can create a new emotion. You've heard the expression, "Fake it 'til you make it." Well, this is precisely what you are doing. You have to surrender to that emotion, which is powerful and strong. Changing your emotions takes time. The BEST way to surrender to an emotion, is to acknowledge it, observe it, sit with it for a few minutes, and consider what you are telling yourself. Once you understand these things, you can then change that dialogue so that you can get a new emotional response. I find that works best by developing a mantra. You must create a new thought pattern, or a new story, in order to trigger your brain to create a new chemical reaction, which is that new emotion. A mantra that is continually repeated will help drive out that negative thought that is causing the emotion you want to change. In our example, that emotion we identified was fear. This is how you make a decision to change your emotions and get a new emotional response. It does not happen instantly. But it does happen faster than you might think. I like short repeatable mantras that are easy to remember and can be chanted under my breath. In this case, you might chant something like, "I will listen to my horse, I will dismount if I need to." I like to use positive thoughts, so instead of chanting, "I won't' fall off of my horse" I'd recommend something positive, "I will dismount if needed." When I say, "chant your mantra," I mean it. Chant it over and over again, a million times if necessary. Keep chanting until you feel your emotions changing, and the fear subsiding. Then keep going. Chant through the entire parade, if needed.

Don't wait until a parade to try this emotional response training. Start it today by observing your emotions, and changing your thinking. Today, as you are going about your day, promise yourself the next time you feel frustrated, you will try this. For example, let's say that sometime today your husband, who promised to mow the lawn, didn't do it, and you are annoyed. Observe your feelings. You feel annoyed. Ask yourself, why are you feeling annoyed and frustrated? Ask yourself, what is the internal story? That story unfolds to, "My husband is being lazy, today. I was counting on him. Now, I probably have to do it, and I'm busy and tired." Let's say that is your internal story. Can you see how that story would trigger the emotion of frustration? What if the reason he didn't mow the lawn, is that he tried to, but the mower wouldn't start, and was broken down.You didn't know that. Would that instantly change your emotions? It might! Has that happened to you, where you find out some circumstance, and it immediately changes your feelings? Why don't we give others the benefit of the doubt? What if instead of believing our husband was intentionally avoiding work, instead we believed he had something come up, that prohibited him from mowing?

When we get intentional about giving people the benefit of the doubt, it not only changes our emotional reaction to things, but it also doesn't rob our present state of happiness. So in this soliloquy, what might your new internal story become? I would suggest something like this, "I bet my husband is really tired today, maybe the mower broke down, maybe he forgot it needed to get done, I hope he is okay, and not too stressed out about work or something." Changing that dialogue puts you in a place of compassion, and it doesn't rob you of your peace right now.

You might be thinking, "It's all a lie, I'm lying to myself, my husband really is a lazy person that doesn't contribute enough." My reply to you is, "So what? It's not like you can control other people, anyway. All you can do is control yourself." By controlling yourself and your own emotions, you won't rob yourself of your peace and happiness, right now. I ask you, is there a possibility that the new dialogue, that new story, could be true? Is there a sliver of hope that it could be true? Then why not gift that possibility to the other person, whether they deserve it or not. Ultimately it is your peace of mind that is on the line. By ruminating on negative thoughts, and allowing those negative feelings to stir and churn, you are setting yourself up for rage, anger, bitterness, and resentment. Good emotional reactions do not stem from those strong feelings. The stronger the feelings, the more likely we are to also exhibit a physical response. Who hasn't trembled in fear, or shook with rage, or had an upset stomach when sad, or experienced tears of joy? Emotional reactions can be powerfully strong. That's why I really believe in mantras. It's a way to stew and churn in positive thoughts.

Here is the process:

1. Observe your emotions (big emotions may take some meditation to consider what your internal story might be).
2. Discover your internal story or dialogue
3. Change your internal story to something positive
4. Create a mantra from that new internal story
5. Chant your mantra and wait for your brain to catch up with a new emotional response.

Let's consider for a moment the idea of meditation. I don't know about you, but I imagine meditation as someone sitting in lotus position, eyes closed, in a flower garden somewhere. But meditation can happen in smaller, yet intentional, ways. A friend of mine who has severe anxiety says taking a few big deep breaths helps her when she is feeling anxious. Sometimes she takes a small walk to try and expel some nervous energy, she's even been known to drink a little water or have a small snack to help settle the physical reaction she gets from her emotions. These are meditative acts. You are taking a small time-out to think about your situation. I challenge you though with the idea that instead of getting sucked into a vortex of negativity, that you really dive and ask yourself what your internal story is. That is at the heart of making positive changes. Practice it today. You can practice this with any emotion: happiness, fear, sadness, anger, anxiety. Remember, observe your emotions, ask yourself what you are telling yourself, develop a new mantra and be patient and wait for a new emotion.

Remember, you can't control others. You can't even control your own horse, honestly. You can control what you do, and what your decisions are. If your horse is having a meltdown, what will you do about that? You can't necessarily calm down your horse, but you can decide if your horse has a meltdown, and is inconsolable, you'll stuff them back on the horse trailer and take them home. That may be the new story you tell yourself. So instead of ruminating with anxiety that your horse might freak out (and your worry might actually trigger that) your new internal dialogue will be, "I trust myself to make the right decisions, I'll take my horse home if I need to."

Don't underestimate the power of a good mantra. If they don't work, why do so many professional athletes use them? They use them to combat negativity, to stay focused, to stay in the moment, and to push through their obstacles. I used to compete in triathlons, and I learned first hand the power of focusing on a mantra. A couple of my favorites are, one-step one breath. To me that meant, stay in this moment, don't focus on what you just finished, or how bad or good that last leg of the race went. Just move forward, one step at a time, one breath at a time. Another favorite mantra of mine was, keep moving forward, it doesn't matter how fast, just move forward. I chanted these two mantras in every single race, often switching them out depending on what part of the race I was in. Staying in the current moment, is a powerful way to stay focused, and get out of your own mind-trap of worry. You can't change the past, you can't control what others do in anything, really. However, you can control your actions, your thoughts, and ultimately your emotions.

Whew! That was a lot of heavy thinking to prepare yourself and your horse for a parade! Wow right?! As a riding instructor, triathlete, and horse trainer, I personally have experienced, or witnessed, many of the emotional hurdles riders like you might be experiencing getting ready for your equestrian events. Don't lose sight of what's important here. I often ask my students, "Are you training for the Olympics? No? Then stop being so hard on yourself, and have some fun already." If we aren't having fun, then why are we training in this sport anyway? I also take the last 2 minutes of my riding lessons and tell my students to walk around the arena, and pet their horse, and tell them they were a good horse. Love them, and thank them for the ride. Any ride that we have that didn't result in an accident is a great ride, not a good ride, a great ride. We never know when our last ride will be. We never know when our last moment in life will be. By expressing simple gratitude for what we are getting to experience in our lives, that too can center-us in the moment. Our entire lives are lived in this moment with reflections on past memories and hopes of what we can do in the future. Yet we are guaranteed no future, and the past is behind us. We only have this moment, right now! And we can spend this moment, right now, reflecting on the past and believing the best or worst about our future (understanding that the outcome will likely land in some kind of average result) yet we fret about the extremes.

Here is something to consider...if we can believe the best or worst about our future, why not choose to believe the absolute best could happen? By borrowing the worst case scenario, we just screw up our present moment of peace. What good is that when we know that the extreme worst case scenario, is not really likely going to come to fruition anyway? Why not believe the best thing is going to happen? When we borrow the best possible outcome, it makes our current moment much more pleasing and enjoyable. The quest for happiness is this discipline of gratitude, and borrowing the positive possibilities that could be our future. So get out there and believe the best in this world, believe the best in your horse, trust yourself to make good decisions, focus on the moment, and go have some fun!

Addendums

Parade Director Question for Parade Reservations

1. Do you have a registration form you need us to fill out?
2. What is the parade director's phone number? Is there a good phone number we can text message on parade day to notify the director we have arrived, or in the event there is an issue that needs attention?
3. What is the address for the parade lineup (nearest business to parade line up for a google address)?
4. What time is the parade lineup?
5. What time does the parade start?
6. May our team be the last in the parade?
7. Where is horse trailer parking? Some of our rigs are 50 foot long bumper to bumper, is there adequate turn around space for rigs?
8. Is there a safe location for horses to be tied up to trailers and readied for the parade- away from traffic? (Not along a roadside or major driveway where cars are going by.)
9. Is a pooper scooper required for this event?
10. Is there someone to escort the horses back to the parade start if the parade is not in a loop? If so, who are we looking for, are they in a ATV, golf cart or police? Will they be able to hold back traffic while our horses cross any streets?

ASA Parade Policy

The American Sidesaddle Association has won numerous awards throughout the years and has even earned money engaging in parades. We have an excellent reputation to maintain, and we ask that all ASA Chapters, Affiliates and members follow our guidelines for both rider and equine safety, along with spectator safety. By adhering to these guidelines, we present a neat and professional appearance,and we show our respect to the parade organizers, media, volunteers, and fellow units. The emphasis is on team work and uniformity, and each point below is important, and thus are in no particular order.

The rider will be required to sign, stating they have read and will follow these guidelines.

Venue Respect

1. Riders will clean up after their horses at parade line up and leave the area as clean as they found it.
2. Riders will make a good effort to provide a side walker and a clean-up person, to pick up droppings along the parade route, showing good sportsmanship by also picking up after non ASA horses that might be in the parade.
3. Spectator Safety
4. Riders will not allow spectators to ride, pet or feed their horses during a parade. It is okay to allow spectators to pet a horse before or after a parade if that spectator is wearing good footwear and the horse is under good emotional control and wearing a halter and leadrope.
5. Due to ASA's insurance, physical interaction with the

crowd is not allowed. Riders are encouraged to smile, wave, talk, and cheer to the crowd, but riders are not allowed to fall out of formation to approach the crowd. Spectators are not allowed to pet or feed horses. If a spectator approaches a rider, it is the duty of the rider to notify a safety walker, parade volunteer/official, or police officer.
6. Costume Rules
7. The individual should make no effort to distinguish themselves above the other team members. The presentation of the unit as a whole, is key to a successful performance. The audience should remember the American Sidesaddle Association, not an individual rider.
8. Cooperation, such as sharing skills and assets like braiding, sewing, labor, or trailering, is paramount. The close knit nature of our group is one of the hallmarks of our success.
9. To prevent any confusion on costuming, team leaders or parade coordinators should provide a list of guidelines or color schemes. If there is a costume committee, guidelines should be released at the earliest convenience, based on when a venue/festival makes announcements of any theme. The costuming committee or coordinator will be named on the guidelines, so to allow members to reach out with questions and clarifications.
10. Going forward, a costume committee or coordinator may require a photo of horse and rider in costume two weeks to a month before the date of the parade, at the discretion of the costume coordinator. A photo of the pieces of costume may be accepted. Spot checks will also be made in the line up area, and the costume coordinator reserves the right to ask an individual to alter, add, or remove an item in their costume.
11. Skirts should be full enough to drape safely around side-

saddle horns, you may open a seam and add velcro for extra safety, you may use a matching apron and pretty top instead of a dress. Make sure you are using a safety release stirrup for sidesaddle.
12. Glitter on hooves is encouraged or bell boots or hoof boots in glitter to match costumes, ribbons or flowers in mane and tail to match costume is encouraged, you may use garlands to match, if appropriate for the costume guidelines.
13. Please keep accessories to those that do not hang down or pose a potential hazard while riding. Scarves, if worn, should be pinned and not tied around the neck.
14. Some parade venues ask that we wear their show ribbons on our bridles on the left, where the browband meets the cheek piece. This is part of being a uniform team. If your horse doesn't like this, please practice at home before parade day. Parade horses need to be able to tolerate a lot of things and this should not be too much for them. Only if your horse has an eye injury can the ribbon be placed an inch down the throat latch.
15. Lineup Responsibilities
16. A rider's horse must be clean and presentable to ride in any parade. It is the rider's responsibility to make sure the horse they are riding is bathed and groomed before the parade or any rehearsal and/or meeting. If an individual is leasing a horse, they should arrive on time to get the horse ready. It is also considerate to contribute to fuel reimbursement if trailer hauling was not part of the lease fee.
17. If there is a mounted rehearsal and safety briefing, being on time is vital. As a rider you will receive your riding position and instruction. If a rider is late or unable to attend, they risk being excluded from the parade.
18. At a parade meeting or rehearsal, a rider will be given

their line up position. Please respect that this is based on certain criteria and may change from time to time as new horses and riders are added. Positions are based on safety, and a solid team appearance. If there is a safety concern, a rider is welcome to bring it up with the parade coordinator. If asking to swap positions, both riders must be in agreement, and present it to the parade coordinator; however, the riders must respect the coordinator's final decision.
19. Please try to put one experienced parade rider in each row. Once on the parade route, please listen to this rider. It is understood that even solid parade horses can have a bad day. However, the harder all riders work to be a team, the better the unit looks. All these things can be practiced at home with a few friends.

Rider Responsiblities

1. If a horse is growing upset, some parades may have a veterinarian who will administer sedatives. Please listen to the horse. If a horse is upset, dismount and hand walk the horse, or remove it from the parade for the safety of everyone. Once on the parade route, if a horse is upset and agitated, a safety walker may elect to lead that horse for group safety. A rider may also ask for help from the safety walkers. A horse that is dancing, bug eyed, agitated, and upset could be a safety issue, and it also does not present a good image for ASA, therefore it is important to listen to the horse and remove it from the parade.
2. Once on the parade route, all riders must maintain their assigned position. For safety and team appearance, spacing between rows and lines must be kept even. This

means that a rider may need to check or urge their horse forward as to not fall out of place. No horse should be ahead or behind, as the spacing between rows is for safety. Horses will either be side by side in a pair of two, or single file.
3. Horses will be kept at least one horse length apart. The horse length is determined by the size of the horse one is riding. The bigger the horse, the more space that is required.
4. In smaller parades, turning to the crowd when stopped can be a nice thing. But in the bigger parades, the ASA unit may be too large to handle this safely. If you are in a large group of horses and the parade stops, keep your horse straight in its row. Do not turn your horse's haunches towards the crowd or another rider.
5. If a spectator approaches a rider, it is the duty of the rider to notify a safety walker, parade volunteer, or police officer. The only exception to this clause is during the Preview Party for the Pegasus Parade. In this situation, the horse must be restrained and under direct control of a handler (halter and lead, bridle and reins, in the hands of the handler), behind the fence. No member of the audience is allowed to be inside the fence or to sit on the horse. Saddles should be kept in direct sight of Preview Party booth workers, with all safety precautions being taken. ASA could be found liable for injury if a guest were to fall off a saddle or have a lightweight stand collapse. For this reason, ASA's insurance strongly advises against allowing guests to sit in saddles, on or off the horse.
6. Riders must have previous parade experience riding aside, or have a recommendation from an ASA instructor.
7. Riders must listen to side walkers who are there for

the safety of the team. Side walkers are responsible for helping to keep spectators back if needed, and to assist riders. If a rider is out of line-up, the side walker is there to help provide support and direction.
8. Youth/Junior Members
9. Sidesaddle riders must have excellent riding skills, have ridden aside in previous public appearances, and have a parent or guardian with them in the parade either mounted or on foot. Astride riders must also have excellent riding skills. Astride riders also must have a parent or guardian with them in the parade either mounted or on foot.
10. Riders 18 years of age or younger must wear an ASTM/SEI helmet and there will be a label inside the helmet that states same. Safety derbies and safety western hats are not acceptable for ASA junior riders in parades.
11. Minors must be accompanied to the event and observed by at least two adults at all times.
12. No junior riders may ride a stallion.
13. Junior members must have a tack safety check by an adult before mounting.
14. Rider Selection
15. Riders may be limited to 21 people in a parade event. A backup list may be kept by the parade coordinator in case of cancellations. Rider selection will be based on previous attendance, teamwork, history, and other criteria to be determined by the costume committee. Anyone not selected to ride is encouraged to participate as a safety walker or ground crew. Those having performed those duties in the past will be given some priority over those who have never attended. In ASA, side walkers, grooms, and other crew are also earning participation points.
16. Horse Rules

17. All horses must have previous parade or major event experience before being ridden sidesaddle in a parade.
18. Please notify the parade coordinator in advance if you are bringing a stallion. Be advised, stallions (even if well behaved or proven to get along with mares and geldings) are forbidden in most parades.
19. Lame or sore horses are not allowed. Horses must be in good condition, in addition to having a health certificate from a veterinarian (for parades where horses are traveling across state lines). A negative coggins test is usually required for every parade. Your parade coordinator will state the parameters of when tests are required.
20. It is recommended that riders have ridden their parade mount prior to rehearsals, if possible.
21. Any horse or rider deemed unsafe prior to lineup may be excused from the unit. This will be the decision of the parade committee, coordinators or an ASA team leader.
22. Tack Rules
23. All tack must be in clean and in safe working condition; no faded nylon or rusty equipment. A responsible adult must double check all junior riders' tack.
24. All sidesaddles must have a leaping horn. The sidesaddle must be fitted (shimmed in necessary) to fit the horse comfortably. Balance girths must be used.
25. Make sure you are using a safety release stirrup; especially for a sidesaddle.
26. Riders need to double check their tack before mounting.
27. English or Western sidesaddle may have a bridle that has bling to match. Please use a noseband (English style or western tie down), rope halter, or leather halter in case a horse needs to be led during the parade.
28. Saddle pad, if used, should match the costume. Bling is encouraged (depending on the costume theme), and a breastcollar is optional.

29. Bridles may be traditional leather or bio/nylon to match the costume. Please use a noseband.
30. Blinker hoods are allowed; if your horse has never used blinkers, consider removing the plastic cups from the hood or practice at home.
31. Wave, smile, and follow the costume guidelines. Have fun!

Made in the USA
Middletown, DE
16 February 2025